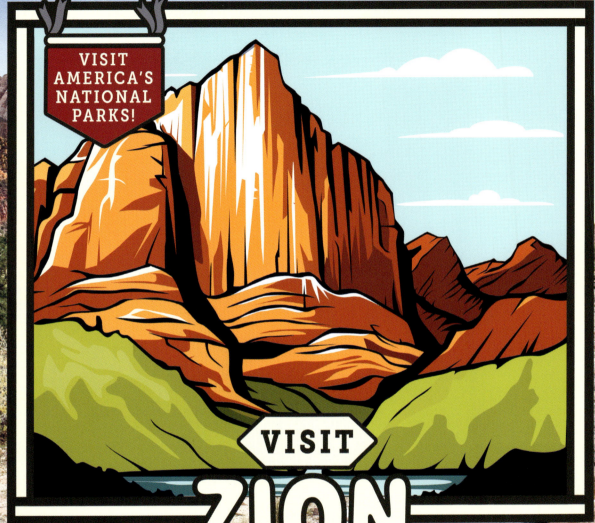

BY SLOANE GOULD

VISIT AMERICA'S NATIONAL PARKS!

VISIT ZION NATIONAL PARK!

Enslow PUBLISHING

Please visit our website, www.enslow.com. For a free color catalog of all our high-quality books, call toll free 1-800-398-2504 or fax 1-877-980-4454.

Cataloging-in-Publication Data

Names: Gould, Sloane.
Title: Visit Zion National Park! / Sloane Gould.
Description: Buffalo, NY : Enslow Publishing, 2026. | Series: Visit America's national parks! | Includes glossary and index.
Identifiers: ISBN 9781978544277 (pbk.) | ISBN 9781978544284 (library bound) | ISBN 9781978544291 (ebook)
Subjects: LCSH: Zion National Park (Utah)–Juvenile literature.
Classification: LCC F832.Z8 G685 2026 | DDC 979.2'48–dc23

Published in 2026 by
Enslow Publishing
2544 Clinton Street
Buffalo, NY 14224

Copyright © 2026 Enslow Publishing

Designer: Tanya Dellaccio Keeney
Editor: Caitie McAneney

Photo credits: Cover (background) Daniel Rose/Shutterstock.com; cover (illustration) ideapaad66/Shutterstock.com; p. 5 (top) Calin Tatu/Shutterstock.com; p. 5 (bottom) Ryan Kelehar/Shutterstock.com; p. 7 (top) OLOS/Shutterstock.com; p. 7 (bottom) Cheri Alguire/Shutterstock.com; p. 9 (top) Brocreative/Shutterstock.com; p. 9 (bottom) Mike Frye/Shutterstock.com; p. 11 Pedro Carrilho/Shutterstock.com; p. 13 LouieLea/Shutterstock.com; p. 15 (top) Martin M303/Shutterstock.com; p. 15 (bottom) Carlos R Cedillo/Shutterstock.com; p. 17 Wyatt Rivard/Shutterstock.com; p. 19 (top) Randy Andy/Shutterstock.com; p. 19 (bottom) Jakub Maculewicz/Shutterstock.com; p. 21 Simone Hogan/Shutterstock.com.

All rights reserved. No part of this book may be reproduced in any form without permission in writing from the publisher, except by a reviewer.

Some of the images in this book illustrate individuals who are models. The depictions do not imply actual situations or events.

Printed in the United States of America

CPSIA compliance information: Batch #CSENS26: For further information contact Enslow Publishing at 1-800-398-2504.

CONTENTS

AMAZING ZION 4

EXPLORE THE HISTORY 6

CANYONS ALL AROUND! 8

ZION CANYON 10

ZION BIOMES 12

AT HOME IN ZION 14

TAKE A HIKE 16

WHAT A VIEW! 18

ADVENTURE AWAITS 20

GLOSSARY 22

FOR MORE INFORMATION 23

INDEX 24

Words in the glossary appear in **bold** type the first time they are used in the text.

AMAZING ZION

Zion National Park has a landscape that's out of this world! People visit this park to explore its deep canyons, desert and forest areas, and wonderful water **features**.

This park is a great place for hikers. Some hikes are so difficult that people need to get a **permit** before trying them. Others are easy enough for families to hike together. With around 146,600 acres (59,327 ha), this park gives visitors a taste of the natural landscape of southwestern Utah.

MORE TO KNOW
Around 4.6 million people visit Zion National Park each year!

ANGELS LANDING

Angels Landing is a major **attraction** in the park, but people need a permit to climb it.

EXPLORE THE HISTORY

People have moved through and lived in this area for thousands of years. Native peoples created rich **cultures** here. The peoples of Zion National Park include the Southern Paiute and Puebloans.

In the 1800s, white settlers started putting down roots in the area. It was settled by Mormons who were looking for a land to practice their religion. People wanted to **protect** the wildness of the landscape. It was made into a national park in 1919.

MORE TO KNOW
Mormons follow a special kind of Christianity that was founded in the 1820s. Many belong to the Church of Jesus Christ of Latter-day Saints (LDS Church).

The Human History Museum of Zion National Park gives visitors a look at Native cultures and Mormon settlers.

CANYONS ALL AROUND!

Canyons are large cuts in the earth with steep sides. Canyons often have rivers running through them. Zion National Park has many canyons made of sedimentary rock, such as sandstone. They have different bands of color that show the different **layers** of rock.

Some people like to hike the rim, or edges, of wider canyons. Others like to walk through slot canyons. These canyons have steep sides with very narrow, or thin, pathways between them.

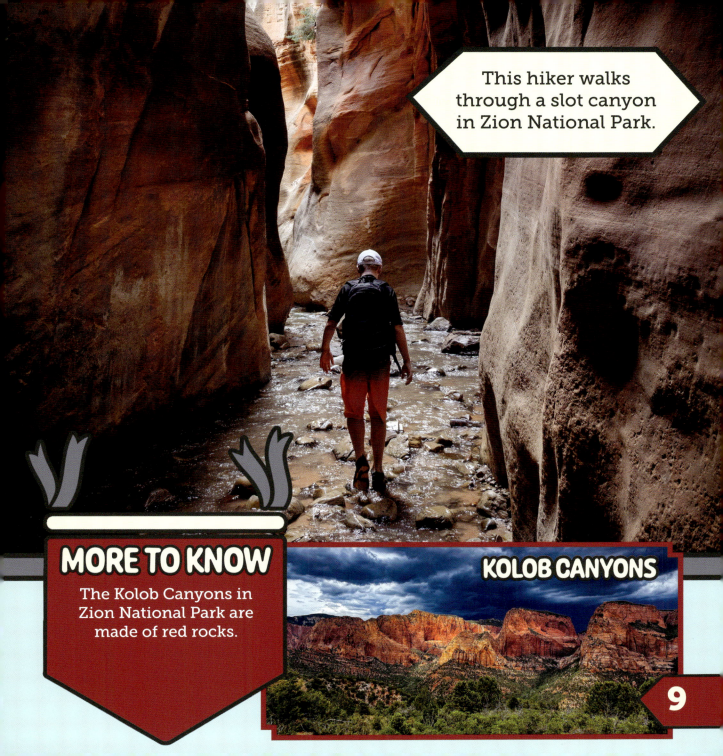

This hiker walks through a slot canyon in Zion National Park.

MORE TO KNOW

The Kolob Canyons in Zion National Park are made of red rocks.

KOLOB CANYONS

ZION CANYON

Zion Canyon is one of the main attractions of the park. Some parts of this canyon are almost 3,000 feet (914 m) deep! That's more than a half-mile drop.

This canyon was carved by the Virgin River millions of years ago. The steep walls of the canyons rise up on either side of the river. The narrowest section is called The Narrows. Many people hike through The Narrows, which involves getting a little wet in the river.

This is the view of Zion Canyon from Canyon Overlook trail in Zion National Park.

MORE TO KNOW

Zion Canyon is 15 miles (24 km) long.

ZION BIOMES

There are three major **biomes** in Zion National Park: desert, forest, and wetland. In lower **elevations**, there's a desert biome. The ground is very dry and the temperature is often very hot. The few plants that grow here include desert shrubs and cacti.

In the higher-elevation **plateaus**, forests of tall pine and fir trees cover the land. The wet, rich area along the Virgin River is also full of plant life. Here, you'll find green grasses, mosses, and huge cottonwood trees.

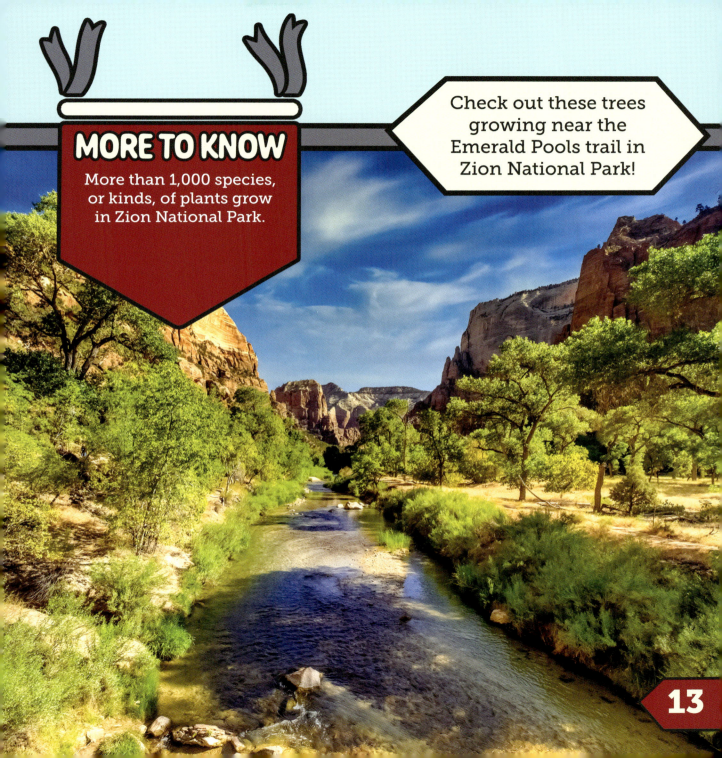

MORE TO KNOW

More than 1,000 species, or kinds, of plants grow in Zion National Park.

Check out these trees growing near the Emerald Pools trail in Zion National Park!

AT HOME IN ZION

Nearly 70 species, or kinds, of **mammals** live in Zion National Park. Some are small, like kangaroo rats and rock squirrels. Others are large, such as bighorn sheep and mountain lions. Most desert animals are nocturnal, or active at night. That's a helpful **adaptation** where it is hot and dry.

Zion is also home to many different species of reptiles, from tiny lizards to deadly rattlesnakes. The Great Basin rattlesnake doesn't need water for months at a time, which is a great adaptation.

Condors are rare, large birds that live in Zion National Park.

MORE TO KNOW

The ringtail cat is a nocturnal animal found in Zion National Park.

TAKE A HIKE

Zion National Park has more than 90 miles (145 km) of hiking trails! Some are good for beginners, such as the Lower Emerald Pools Trail. A short hike brings you to Emerald Pools and surrounding waterfalls.

Other hikes are very hard! You need to be in good shape and have the right gear. The West Rim trail involves a lot of climbing. One of the hardest hikes is through The Narrows. This trail is 16 miles (26 km) long and some of it involves swimming!

The Subway is a difficult hike through a slot canyon.

MORE TO KNOW

Backpacking is hiking plus camping overnight. These hikes take more than one day.

17

WHAT A VIEW!

Many people come to Zion National Park for the views. Some views are easy to get to by car, with parking lots nearby. For example the Canyon Overlook Trail includes a great view of the Pine Creek slot canyon.

The Riverside Walk gives people a view of the Virgin River. It's also the starting point for The Narrows hike. The view at Big Bend gives visitors a look at the rocky beauty of Angels Landing, Cable Mountain, and the Great White Throne.

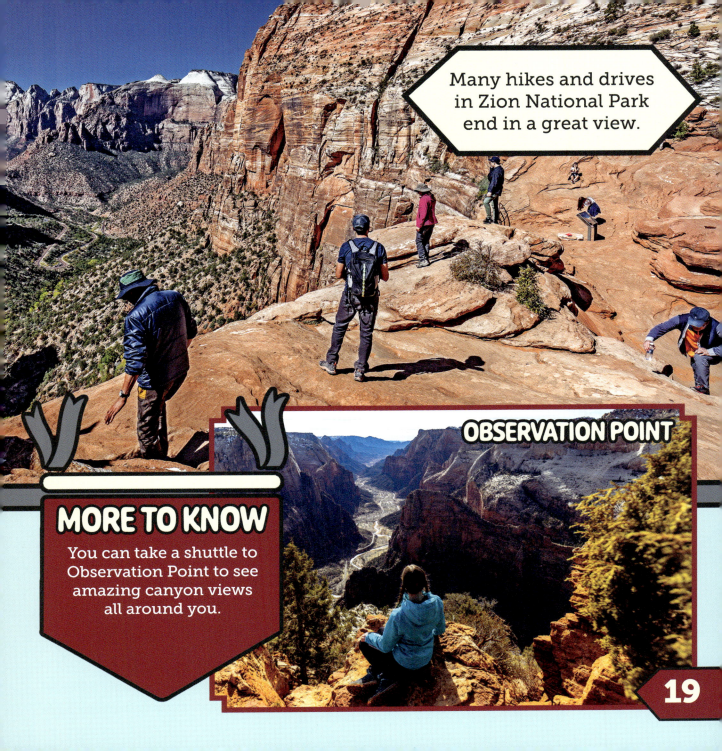

Many hikes and drives in Zion National Park end in a great view.

OBSERVATION POINT

MORE TO KNOW

You can take a shuttle to Observation Point to see amazing canyon views all around you.

19

ADVENTURE AWAITS

Zion National Park has activities for everyone! While some people like driving around, others like hiking. Still others take horseback rides through wilderness or bike on roads through the park.

Zion is a great place to camp. The stars are beautiful at night away from city lights. It's also a great place to watch animals, such as birds. This national park blends the beauty of the desert with cool canyons and forests. What would you like to do there?

People bike using the Pa'rus Trail in Zion National Park.

MORE TO KNOW

Zion National Park has three campgrounds to choose from. Some people camp in tents and others camp in RVs.

GLOSSARY

adaptation: Changes in the body or behavior that help an animal live in their environment, or surroundings.

attraction: Something people travel to see.

biome: A natural community of plants and animals, such as a forest or desert.

culture: The beliefs and ways of life of a group of people.

elevation: Height above sea level.

feature: An interesting or important part, look, or way of being.

layer: One thing lying over or under another.

mammal: A warm-blooded animal that has a backbone and hair, breathes air, and feeds milk to its young.

permit: A piece of paper that allows someone to do something.

plateau: A large area of land with raised sides and a level top.

protect: To keep safe.

FOR MORE INFORMATION

Books

Bowman, Chris. *Zion National Park.* Minneapolis, MN: Bellwether Media, 2023.

Siber, Kate. *National Parks of the U.S.A.* London, UK: Wide Eyed Editions, 2024.

Websites

Utah
kids.nationalgeographic.com/geography/states/article/utah
Explore the state of Utah—home to Zion National Park.

Zion National Park
kids.britannica.com/kids/article/Zion-National-Park/489272
Learn more fun facts about Zion National Park.

Publisher's note to educators and parents: Our editors have carefully reviewed these websites to ensure that they are suitable for students. Many websites change frequently, however, and we cannot guarantee that a site's future contents will continue to meet our high standards of quality and educational value. Be advised that students should be closely supervised whenever they access the internet.

INDEX

adaptations, 14

Angels Landing, 5, 18

animals, 14, 15, 20

attractions, 5, 10

backpacking, 17

biomes,

culture, 6, 7

elevation, 12

Emerald Pools, 13, 16

hiking, 4, 8, 10, 16, 17, 19

Human History Museum of Zion National Park, 7

Kolob Canyons, 9

Mormons, 6, 7

Narrows, The, 10, 16, 18

Observation Point, 19

plants, 12, 13

Puebloans, 6

Riverside Walk, 18

sedimentary rock, 8

slot canyons, 8, 9, 18

Southern Paiute peoples, 6

Subway, The, 17

Utah, 4

Virgin River, 10, 12, 18

Zion Canyon, 10, 11